The Enneagram

Learn the 9 Personality Types for Healthy Relationships; a Complete Guide to Self-Realization & Self-Discovery Using the Wisdom of the Enneagram: Best Enneagram Audiobooks & Books; Book 1

By Carly Greene

Table of Contents

Introduction

Since the beginning of time, people have always felt that they need to understand themselves better. As humans, we have often cast our curiosity upon the world around us, asking how it behaves and what it is made of. But nothing has been as interesting to us as what makes us human. To understand the experiences of being human and the things that make us behave as we do is an honorable quest. In our journey, we have always wondered what makes people different, what makes us unique, and how we fit in the world. The Enneagram is a personality typing system that is a part of that story. In it, we find nine personality types which are interconnected. It is a nuanced and complex system that shows who we are, what motivates us, our deepest fears, our strengths and weaknesses, and what we do at our worst and best. It is exhaustive. Today millions take the test to find out more about themselves, how they relate to others and the world.

Know Thyself

There is a lot to be gained from understanding ourselves. When we understand ourselves, we know how to accurately predict our behavior. Predicting our behavior allows us to make better plans to better position ourselves to get what we want, and put measures in place to prevent us from acting in undesirable ways. Understanding ourselves gives us insight into our behavior. Insight can heal us; it can make us kinder to ourselves, and reveal our truest desires, freeing us from destructive time-wasting habits. We will know what true success looks like to us, what a happy and fulfilled life looks like with this insight. This can save us a lot of pain and lead us to self-acceptance. With an understanding of ourselves, we can discover how we fit in society, what our role in the world is, and how to maximize our potential in that area. These are important things. They are the things that determine how happy and successful we are going to be in our lives. It is important to know ourselves for these reasons. The Enneagram system gives us that opportunity.

In this book, I will explore what those personality types are. I will also spend some time elaborating on various topics that relate to the Enneagram system. Then we will give each type a roadmap to happiness, self-actualization, and completeness. It is going to be a brief journey, but not one without value.

Chapter 1: The Types

In this chapter, we will go over the descriptions of the nine basic personality types found in the Enneagram. First, I will go over some things worth understanding about the Enneagram system and its structure.

The Structure

The personality types that are in the Enneagram system are interconnected and relate to one another in complex ways. To illustrate these connections and relationships, the proponents of the system have devised a structure. This structure is a cycle with the number 9 on top, right where 12 would be on a clock, and evenly spaced around the cycle are the remaining numbers placed clockwise. Each number represents a personality type. Inside the circle, there are lines that connect the numbers in very specific patterns. These lines indicate what are called directions of integration and disintegration. Each type will have two lines emanating from them that connect with two other types. One line will be the direction of integration for that type, and the other will represent the direction of disintegration. These lines tell us what that type is likely to look like when under stress (disintegration) and when things are going well (integration). For instance, a one who is doing well will act as a healthy seven at the same developmental level, and a one who isn't will act like a five of the same developmental level. We will talk more about developmental levels later.

The position that each personality type takes on the cycle is not arbitrary. The personality types flanking a given personality type are generally present within the personality in the middle. These personality types are called wings. When you take an Enneagram personality test, you will be given your dominant personality type as your type. This means the number you are given is the personality type that fits you best. Then you will be given scores about your wings. This will tell you about the secondary personality type which also best represents you, think of this as another side of your personality. You will also get scores about the extent to which you can find yourself in other personality types in the system. People generally have one dominant personality type and a wing. The culmination of these types is the amalgam of your personality. So you will hear some people saying, "I am a one with a nine as a wing." This just tells us the two most dominant personality types within that person. Still, strictly speaking, you can find bits of yourself scattered about the structure. This is why a one can act like a seven in certain situations, but their dominant type is who they are most of the time or deep down.

The numbers given to the types say nothing about whether or not they are better than other types. An eight is not better than a two and vice versa. Even when we talk about the traits belonging to any of the personality types, no one is better than anyone else. However, it may appear so in the real world. The environment may reward certain personalities more than others because they have skills that are highly valued. Still, the opposite can be true in another environment.

All the types in the Enneagram have basic fears and desires. Their desire is the thing they want the most, and their fear is the thing they are terrified of.

Let's turn to our personality types.

Type 1: The Reformer

They are also referred to as the reformer. Type ones have a great sense of right and wrong, and they are driven by a sense of purpose to improve things and the world. They want more than anything to be good. They would easily sacrifice comfort and other things so that they can be an instrument of change. This type is well known for being organized, disciplined, and principled. Ones fear being corrupted and being evil. Since they have such high standards and work hard to uphold them, they can sometimes be critical and express resentment when others get by with little effort. Since they have worked so hard and everything they do is justified in their minds, they can be impatient with others who don't show equal sensitivity or frugality. When ones are at their best, they become like wise gurus. They are discerning, and they inspire great admiration from others through their moral heroism.

Type 2: The Helper

Twos are the most caring, and they show a great deal of empathy and self-sacrifice. They like seeing others happy, they always have good intentions, and they are generous. Because of how much they give and the sacrifices they make, they can have problems with being jealous and with self-neglect. They fear being unwanted and unloved. Their biggest desire is to be loved by others; they want to be needed, valued, and treasured. You will see twos reveling in family closeness, in serving others and giving them attention. They are the most compassionate, helpful, and loving, and they enjoy it. Their generosity is a blessing to those that are fortunate enough to have them in their lives.

Type 3: The Achiever

Threes are driven, and they are focused on being successful. They are filled with ambitions, and they put together pragmatic measures to get what they want. They want to advance in life, so they work hard. At their best, they are role models. They struggle with working too hard and being too competitive, even in places where that may not be needed. They run the risk of being inauthentic because they will chase anything that gives them the self-image they think is of the most value. Since they are sensitive to success and social hierarchies, threes can be self-conscious if they aren't as accomplished as they think they should be. Their biggest fear is being less valuable and being low grade. Their biggest desire in life is to be valuable and to be important and integral to things. They want others to affirm these strong desires, so you will find them reveling in attention and admiration.

Type 4: The Individualist

Type fours are the honest and sensitive type. They have a great deal of self-awareness, they are withdrawn, and they are contemplative. You can describe them as being emotionally bare, personal and expressive. They will not pretend to feel or think what they don't. Because they are so in touch with their emotions, they are prone to depression, wallowing in unpleasant feelings, and self-medicating. They may pull away from others because they feel like there is something wrong with them. They can be highly creative and imaginative. The biggest thing they desire is to just be themselves, be genuine to who they are; that is why they become invested in finding themselves. Their biggest fear is a lack of identity or the inability to make a mark on the world through their disposition.

Type 5: The Investigator

Type fives are driven by a thirst to understand things at their most fundamental level. They are cerebral, curious, and love complex, stimulating things. They can focus for long periods. They easily became detached from others and can withdraw into their minds a lot more easily as they find their inner world a lot more interesting. When fives are at their best, they can break new ground, make people see things a lot differently. Their biggest fear is being incompetent, ignorant, or useless. Their biggest desire is to achieve mastery of whatever thing they invest their time and energy in.

Type 6: The Loyalist

As the name suggests, loyalists are the most loyal of the types. They are very dependable and responsible, work hard, and are always there to ensure that everything is running smoothly. They have an inkling to make sure of this because sixes are security-driven; their biggest desire is to have security and safety. Because this is what they want the most, they can be filled with suspicion and anxiety if they aren't confident that they have security. Their anxiety reveals that their biggest fear is to be without security. So in everything they do, they try to secure it or maintain it. At their best, they're the most stable of citizens, and others go to them to find their strength, they are confident, warm, and self-reliant.

Type 7: The Enthusiast

Sevens are energetic, full of life, and people-loving. They go into the world with lively optimism, energy, and enthusiasm that make them take on new challenges with ease. They are joyous, adaptable, and fun. They can struggle with being impulsive and being able to sustain their efforts for long periods. As a result, they find themselves dabbling here and there, stretching their resources thin. This happens because sevens like exhilarating, novel things. It keeps their spirits high; otherwise, they would become uninterested and drained. Their biggest fear is pain and discomfort, and their greatest desire is to be comfortable and content. At their best, sevens know how to focus their energy, they are infectiously happy and bold.

Types 8: The Challenger

Eights are domineering and assertive. They go into the world, determined to take charge. They can be territorial, bossy, and confrontational. They are known for looking out for themselves first and always trying to take the lead. At their worst, they have a short temper and refuse to be open up to others. They believe vulnerability is a show of weakness, and weakness invites others to take control. Their biggest fear is being under the dominance and control of others, so they are very sensitive to others trying to assume a role like that. Deep down, eights want to be protected, so they try to achieve that by controlling themselves and the environment around them; they want to completely rely on themselves and showcase their strength. At their best, eights are at the top, they lead well, they are free from insecurities, and they display astonishing discipline and self-mastery.

Type 9: The Peacemaker

Nines are the most agreeable and peace-loving of all the types. They look outwards into the world, and they want to create and maintain as much harmony and peace as possible. Because they are trying to preserve peace at all costs, they can go along with things quite easily, becoming supportive and complacent. Because they trust and feel comfortable in the peace that is created. They can be slow to act and refuse any pushes towards change because they deem it unnecessary. In their minds, there is no need to stir things up even if it is for the fun of it - it is all well when all is peaceful. Because they are open-minded, nines at their best display a non-judgmental attitude, and they become excellent conflict fixers. Their biggest fear is being disconnected from others; keeping the peace is their way of preventing this. They desire inner stability and connectedness more than any other type. This is why they display acute spiritual sensitivity.

Chapter 2: Emotions We Find Challenging and How We Deal with Them

If you think of the world as a game that has challenges and can be beaten, personality types are just different strategies for playing that game. No one strategy is inherently better than the other as all of these strategies are proven successful. That is why we still have them in society because nature has selected them. These strategies are a response to three basic challenges. While most of us in life will face the same challenges, some of us will be more affected by some challenges than others. We will struggle against them. Our personalities are the source of our vulnerability to some challenges, just as much as they give us an advantage in other areas. Researchers realized that the personalities in the Enneagram system can be separated into three themes or centers; these tell us which of the main challenges afflicts the personalities in that section. The different personalities deal with that main challenge in distinct ways. This does not mean that the personalities in one section do not face the challenges faced by the other two sections; it just means for them, it isn't as big a driver. Here we will look at three different sections, and we will see how this shows itself within the personalities.

Center 1: The Action/Gut Center

This section comprises personality types one, nine, and eight. The main challenges faced by those in this center are anger and control. It means these two emotions are the most dominant, challenging, or influential compared to the other types. The types deal with this differently.

Nines are the peacemakers, so when they experience anger or a loss of control, they respond to it by denying it or trying to be indifferent to it. They won't say you have made them mad because doing so might escalate things. They think this is a viable way of creating stability.

Eight responds to anger by displaying it. They think that doing so will put them in a commanding position, and they believe they can control the anger. We have seen that this can be problematic, and this is why this type is known for sometimes having problems with their temper.

Ones suppress their anger. This is because in their quest for perfection and with their huge sense of morality, being angry and losing control looks like something that is against purity and perfection. So they suppress it, they swallow anger and intense emotions. They can harbor great resentment and become critical of others who display theirs, unaware that their response to anger is largely innate.

As you may see from how these types have dealt with the pain, there are three basic ways to react to the defining challenge of each center. The first one is positive. It moves in the direction of the emotions or "embraces" that emotion, how eights deal with anger is an example of this because they let anger in. The second response is one of balance or indifference, and nines are the perfect examples of this because they deal with anger by pretending it is not there. The third response is a negative one; the personalities who use this strategy push back at the emotion -- they refuse to let it in or to let it take hold. As we have seen, ones are perfect examples of that strategy. They suppress their anger refusing to let it sway them.

Center 2: The Feeling/Heart Center

The personalities in the feeling center are two, three, and four. The dominant emotion in this center is shame.

Twos deal with their shame in a direction that "embraces" that emotion. Shame is an emotion that tells us that we ought to feel bad about ourselves as a result of something we have done or something that someone has done who is connected to us. So they deal with it by trying to make other people like them or see them in a better light. This is acting in accordance with how this emotion demands us to repent in some way, and the actions taken by twos in this situation are meant to make things well again.

Threes' method of response is one of indifference. Threes don't try to make up or fix things, they simply focus on their project of being even better as people, they press on. Remember that this type is fixated on being successful, so they might avoid those feelings altogether if they don't see how they serve their ultimate goal.

Fours use the negative method to deal with their shame. They push back by focusing on themselves, particularly on the things that make them special. This serves to validate their feelings of being misunderstood and not quite fitting in with the world, so something that should make them feel ashamed gets interpreted as something misunderstood by society. This quickly turns into self-appraisal, which might lead to feelings of inadequacy, but they will deflect that by finding refuge in their creative and unique side.

Center 3: The Thinking/Head Center

The dominant emotion in this center is fear. The personalities found in this section are fives, sixes, and sevens.

Fives deal with fear by using the negative method. Fear demands that we go out and do something about it; this might mean fighting or running. Fives run, they withdraw into their shell and become isolated. They may become extra secretive and unwilling to participate in the world. Remember that fives want to be competitive, so when they are afraid, they feel incompetent. So their way of dealing with it is retreating until they feel that they are competitive again.

Sixes deal with their fears through the method of balance or indifference. This means that they are not as aware and attuned as other types are to the nature of their situation. So they become anxious. So even when they find a path to security, which is what they want the most, they still feel like it is not enough or that something can go wrong. Instead of running or fighting, they turn to things that can calm them or bring them a sense of peace. They treat the symptoms, not the source.

Sevens positively deal with fear; in this context, it means they run in the opposite direction from fives. Fives ran inwards when faced with fear. Sevens run outwards because their fear generally resides inside, waiting for them. So they distract themselves or bury themselves in a long line of experiences, each crafted to keep them away from feelings of discomfort.

Given that both fives and sevens run, the only person doing the fighting here is Sixes. They try to do something about their fear, but they are consumed by it. Fives know what they fear, so they lock themselves away and train themselves until they become convinced they can beat their fear. Sevens know what they fear, and they try to deal with it by living like it is not there, hoping it wanes and disappears.

Some Thoughts About These Strategies

These strategies are not bad in and of themselves, but they help us make much more sense of what is prized by our personalities. We saw that our dominant emotions are dominant because when they are faced by the types, the types become their most salient selves.

Chapter 3: Levels of Development

Within each personality type, there is a growth ladder from immature to maturity. These levels show us what the types look like on their journey to self-actualization or when they fall away from this goal. This is one of the most important developments in the Enneagram because it shows us how people can change and still be the same basic type. If we understand the types correctly, we can quickly see why they develop and regress the way they do. Each type will have tendencies that are poised to drag it back down or up the ladder. In each personality type, nine levels are separated into three broad categories: healthy, average, and unhealthy. Therapists can easily provide counsel and advice to you if they have a clear picture of where you are on the ladder, as each will require the same kind of intervention. The lowest rung on the ladder would be the level nine, and the highest would be level one. Here are the levels below:

- Level 1: The Level of Liberation
- Level 2: The Level of Psychological Capacity
- Level 3: The Level of Social Value
- Level 4: The Level of Imbalance/Social Role
- Level 5: The Level of Interpersonal Control
- Level 6: The Level of Overcompensation
- Level 7: The Level of Violation
- Level 8: The Level of Obsession and Compulsion
- Level 9: The Level of Pathological Destructive (How The System Works — The Enneagram Institute, 2014)

We are going to examine what these levels look like in all of the types we have discussed. Looking at how they manifest will make us better understand the types and, most importantly, see where we are on that ladder. Once we have identified our level of development, we will know what to do to achieve self-actualization. The healthy levels are levels one, two, and three. The average levels are levels four, five, and six. The unhealthy levels are levels seven, eight, and nine.

We will briefly look at what these classifications mean before we examine how they are dealt with. In ego psychology, the self is separated into three parts: the id, the ego, and the superego. The id is the most instinctual part ourselves; it is filled with our most base desires. It is primitive, unreasonable, and represents our underdeveloped selves. A perfect example of the id is babies who have no regard for anything else but the satisfaction of their needs at all costs. The ego develops as the id is challenged by the environment around it. The ego is the decision making part, which tries to use reason, compromise, and other strategies to meet the needs of the ego or the superego. The superego is the social and morally conscious part of ourselves. It is concerned with doing the right thing and getting along with others in the world. The id and the superego both work to influence the decision-making process of the ego.

Thinking about ego psychology is important because, as we will see, the levels roughly resemble this setup. The higher one climbs up the levels, the more aware and objective they become; the word that is commonly used to describe this is "present."

The Healthy Levels

These are the levels where we are most present. Here, people are at their most objective and in tune with the environment. This means we can step away from ourselves and see ourselves from a neutral viewpoint and act in a way that escapes the trappings of our darkest sides. This part can be thought of as the one that closely resembles the superego in ego psychology. It is characterized by a similar awareness of oneself within society.

The Average Levels

The average levels are characterized by a mixture of both healthy and unhealthy characteristics. Here, awareness is building, but the person in this stage still struggles with the darkest, base aspects of their personality. This part closely resembles the ego, because the ego is often in a position of compromise, juggling the needs of both the id and the superego. But unlike in ego psychology, these levels reflect genuine stages of development on our journey, not an aspect of the personality that is always with us. I am merely showing you these similarities so you can better understand what is meant by terms like ego-centric within an Enneagram context (it means the person more resembles the id; not the ego - weirdly enough).

The Unhealthy Levels

The id can be thought of as our most self-absorbed and subjective part of ourselves so less aware or awake. The lower one is on the ladder, the less present; they are consumed with the basest, most aggressive, negative, and raw parts of their personality. In these levels, we resemble the id because we are more abrasive, irrational, and compulsive. When you hear a commentator say that the person more resembles their ego, or that they are ego-centric, that is what they mean. In Enneagram cycles, the term ego is almost synonymous with the darker self, so it follows that our un-reformed, most basic self, is the ego.

Type 1: The Reformer

Unhealthy Levels

Level 9: Here, we see ones being quite cruel and intolerant to those who they perceive as wrongdoers. This is not strange for a type that tries to repress anger. They are prone to depression and other emotional disturbances.

Level 8: We see them preoccupied with the imperfections of others despite themselves acting in very similar ways to those as they judge. This is primarily due to a lack of self-awareness.

Level 7: They are still set in their ways and preach to others about morality. They also become obsessed with the "right" way of the "truth." No one can quite meet their standards, but when they go astray, it is because of some greater reason that justifies it all.

Average Levels

Level 6: Here, we start to see that exceptionalism slip away once they turn their critical attitude not only towards others but towards themselves. It does not make them any less harsh critically or bring their standards down. They still display impatience through scolding and other confrontational behaviors, quick to point out when something is not being done "the right way."

Level 5: Here, we start to see ones become cautious and puritanical. They display this by becoming extremely organized, orderly, and emotionally absent. They apply the same frugality to their emotional impulses.

Level 4: Now, looking at the world around them, they become dissatisfied with its state, and since they are the ones with the highest ideals, they feel a need to go out and shape the word. They turn into activists, pouring themselves into various causes and initiatives to bring about what ought to be.

Healthy Levels

Level 3: Here, we begin to see ones at their best. They become focused on bringing about justice. Their sense of social responsibility comes about in less aggressive ways, ways that are easier for others to receive.

Level 2: We see them with a developed sense of right and wrong, echoed in strong ontological and moral beliefs. They start to display more rationality, and they begin installing balance in their lives.

Level 1: Now, we see the type at its very best. They are very conscious. They are more able to appreciate the way things are and resolve things with nuance and wisdom that was absent before. At this point, they understand the shortcomings or others and the world a lot better, thus giving them the grace to deal with them. They become gurus, inspiring others towards the truth, humanity, and hope.

Type 2: The Helper

Unhealthy Levels

Level 9: They feel used by others, so they stew in anger and resentment. Instead of being confrontational, that anger presents itself as physical health problems.

Level 8: They feel that people owe them for all that they have done, so they demand to be repaid for any favor they have given. This can border on becoming forceful. While this behavior might look like something an eight would do, twos' assertiveness comes from feeling obligated, not because they want to assert control.

Level 7: They guilt-trip others, reminding them of all they have done for them. They may behave in highly deceptive and manipulative ways. Around this time, they speak to others in a way that makes them feel less or unimportant. This comes from the fact that twos feel that the people in their lives are taking them for granted.

Average Levels

Level 6: They begin to feel like they are special, that they bring value to the table. They see themselves as being a lot more helpful and important than they are making themselves come across - of having given the way they gave. They may appear a little pompous and condescending.

Level 5: We start seeing them get more mixed up in the affairs of those in their lives. This is because they want to be needed and feel that they can be depended upon. To do that, they insert themselves in others' lives, drive for more closeness in their relationships, and become possessive. They tire themselves in the process.

Level 4: They shed their more intrusive side, and what is left is the need to please others. This is a new way that they can feel needed and valuable. So they become friendlier, flirtatious, expressive, and present themselves as people with the best of intentions.

Healthy Levels

Level 3: They start to let go of pleasing others so that they may feel important, loved, or needed. They still appreciate the value of being helpful to others. So they continue to be generous and giving, but this time they have let go of entitlement.

Level 2: They start to grow a lot more empathy and compassion. Here we see them taking care of other's needs, being considerate and attentive. This authenticity is a result of learning that to be truly loved, one has to love and not expect anything. From that, they begin to see others clearly as they stop thinking about what they will get out of the things they do for others. So empathy and compassion are cultivated.

Level 1: They are now truly altruistic, having discovered the magic of selflessness. They shower others with unconditional love, and they feel blessed to be in that position.

Type 3: The Achiever

Unhealthy Levels

Level 9: They can express psychopathic behavior, and they are more prone to narcissistic personality disorder. They don't want to see others that are happier or more successful than they are, so they sabotage others.

Level 8: They want to be successful at any cost, so they hide their mistakes and are more likely to practice "fake it until you make it" at the expense of others. It is at this stage where they are their most duplicitous, untrustworthy, and jealous.

Level 7: On their quest for success, they develop exploitative tactics, having learned that betrayal is only effective in the short term. At the same time, opportunism and exploitation can be sustained for far longer. They are still jealous of other people's success.

Average Levels

Level 6: Threes exhibit narcissistic behavior; they believe themselves to be superior to others. They are filled with arrogance. They don't stop promoting themselves and making themselves look and sound more awesome than they are.

Level 5: They begin to worry about their image and how they are seen by others. They turn their attention to things that will facilitate their success. They become hard-working, ensuring that all their steps are guided by pragmatism. During this period of extreme ambition, they lose the ability to sense their emotions because they are always looking forward.

Level 4: In their quest for success, we start to see threes become more obsessed with their performance and productivity. They are already grounded in being pragmatic in their approach to problems. Now, they want to make sure that they are doing them well enough. They are increasingly terrified of failure, having known how hard they work and how hard they have worked. They are prone to workaholism, working after-hours, and taking the work home. They want to get ahead and climb up the social ladder.

Healthy Levels

Level 3: At this stage, they feel like they haven't yet reached their full potential even when they might be more successful than the majority of people in the field they have chosen. Others already look at them with great reverence, but they still feel like there is more they can do, but that feeling does not come from fear of failing. It is now motivated by an interest in themselves and how far they can push themselves.

Level 2: The arrogance and confidence they displayed in the beginning are now replaced by feelings of high self-esteem, grace, and charisma. They are so sure of themselves and who they are. They do not feel the need to be vindictive anymore. They may even be encouraging to others.

Level 1: Feeling like they have explored all they can about themselves and their limits, not to mention feeling proud of themselves, they become self-effacing, giving, gentle, and authentic. They now find a great deal of love and acceptance for themselves.

Type 4: The Individualist

Unhealthy Levels

Level 9: Here, we see fours consumed with feelings of hopelessness; they may also exhibit self-destructive behavior. They are prone to depression and narcissistic personality disorder. They will self-medicate with drugs and alcohol. It might here that they feel alone or like they belong nowhere.

Level 8: They become extremely delusional about themselves, their place in the world, and how others see them. They direct a lot of anger and hate towards themselves. They do not feel like anyone gets their pain, so they push away anyone who is trying to help, believing they are somehow alien and deficient.

Level 7: They are emotionally numb. From the outside, they look depressed, fatigued, and find it difficult to function. They withdraw from others, but what is different here is that they are not consumed by feelings of self-hate, although they may still harbor a great deal of anger towards themselves.

Average Levels

Level 6: They are convinced they are different from others. This tells them that they can't be held to the same standards as everybody else. So living as everybody does starts to feel like a chore and restraint. To escape, they self-indulge or delve deep into their rich inner world, becoming further removed from everybody else.

Level 5: They are still emotionally sensitive and raw, but now they are becoming a lot more self-conscious. However, they find it difficult to fully immerse themselves in what is going on around them. They are extremely sensitive and are influenced by everything said around them. They drink the world instead of becoming a major participant in it. This makes them moody and increasingly unsure of themselves.

Level 4: They turn to art for salvation, whether by creating or consuming. They make their experience of it much deeper, embed in it more significance and importance than someone else would. It doesn't have to be art, it just has to be something that allows them to examine and interact with their feelings for long periods. This can show itself as other passions like gaming.

Healthy Levels

Level 3: They are now true themselves; they discard all their negative feelings about themselves. They begin embracing themselves as they are. This type of maturity comes from a great deal of emotional strength. It has been crafted through years of allowing themselves to feel.

Level 2: They become self-aware and much more aware of their feelings, now they are able to clearly know where one begins, where the other ends, and why. They have a much better hold on them, unlike in the beginning when they sometimes felt like they alone were in charge.

Level 1: Here, they are at their best; they now manage to fulfill their creative edge. They feel empowered to take on anything, and they can experience things with more richness and appreciation than anyone else. They can find creative ways of turning experiences, even those that are uncomfortable, into wondrous things that should be appreciated and enjoyed. This is because they now have a vast emotional lexicon; they can appreciate all kinds of nuances.

Type 5: The Investigator

Unhealthy Levels

Level 9: At this point, fives may even feel like they do not exist. They feel utterly unformed, and they may feel crushed by the world around them. And so they become suicidal or engage in self-destructive behavior.

Level 8: They are completely enamored by their ideas, but they feel like their mind has a mind of its own, which breeds anxiety. Their minds explore horrible things, things that scare them or even disturb them. They can feel frightened by their mind at this stage.

Level 7: Here, we see fives isolate themselves because of this, and they become even farther away from others. They are ill-equipped socially and are uninterested in learning to interact socially, so they push others away who try to get into their lives. They also retreat into their thoughts and theories because they find them more interesting.

Average Levels

Level 6: We see fives protecting their inner world. They start to practice their intellectual flare by becoming argumentative. Sometimes, they hold views that are extreme or controversial just because of the intellectual vigor of it all. They hate it when people distract them from this pursuit.

Level 5: They begin their affair with increasingly complex ideas. This causes them to become withdrawn.

Level 4: They think carefully before acting on anything. Exploring things in their mind with all their different permutations gives them the confidence they need to act. This makes them good researchers and good forecasters. Because of all this, they develop a mistrust of accepting things at first glance as they have learned how things change under careful observation. As a result, they test ideas and challenge set traditions and wisdom.

Healthy Levels

Level 3: Their love for knowledge and their adventurous bent has now attracted them to one thing that is of great interest to them. They focus on developing mastery in that subject, spending hours, days, months, and even years in that pursuit. During this time, they develop highly original ways of thinking and they become independent.

Level 2: Now that they have acquired all that knowledge, they look at the world around them with an extraordinarily perceptive mind, able to pull things apart to their most fundamental workings. Once they have done this, they can come to incredible insights and predictions. Nothing gets by them.

Level 1: Now that they have amassed that much knowledge and experience, they become open-minded, and they become inventive and drive the respective fields they are in forward.

Type 6: The Loyalist

Unhealthy Levels

Level 9: At their worst, they are self-destructive and suicidal, just like fives. They try to escape all of these intense feelings through drugs and alcohol and other destructive means. This is because their anxious feelings and paranoia get so overbearing that they find taking substances decreases the pain.

Level 8: They feel attacked by others, so they turn to violence and aggressiveness to protect themselves. This behavior might seem irrational, but within their psyche, security comes from those that support, and something outwardly challenging doesn't look like something that can act in their best interest.

Level 7: Here, they are afraid that their behavior sabotages the little support and security they have and panic. This panic makes them unstable, and they feel themselves to be without safety, so they seek other sources of security.

Average Levels

Level 6: They feel insecure, so they become reactionary and divisive. Doing this makes them look tough, and toughness hides their vulnerability. This vulnerability makes them too eager to point the finger at others.

Level 5: Here, they become a mixture of different impulses - the impulse to resist and the impulse to assert their strength. Because of this, they resort to passive aggressiveness and look to be indecisive, and they take a while to complete a task. This happens because they are still unsure of their security, whether from others or their ability to provide it for themselves. So they are still trying to figure themselves out.

Level 4: Now, they have some idea about where they are and what they can do to achieve complete security. They then spend their energy and time trying to attain it. They may become very organized, structured. This change shows just how keen they are for things to go well because, for them, it is their entire well-being at stake, their sense of purpose itself.

Healthy Levels

Level 3: They become hard-working and give their time and resources to institutions, people, and communities that provide and sustain security and safety. They show just how socially constructive they can be.

Level 2: They form strong relationships with others, built on trust and openness. Because of this, many people find them enamoring, and they quickly feel safe in their company.

Level 1: They are completely independent, but they refuse to be completely uninvolved in the world and the lives of others if their support is needed. As a result, they appear to be interdependent, but they are cooperative out of the goodness of their own heart. Here they can easily take leadership roles or move into senior positions. They are a well of stability and wisdom.

Type 7: The Enthusiast

Unhealthy Levels

Level 9: They are prone to feelings of depression, and they become suicidal. In their case, their emotional instability at this stage is dangerous because it is mixed with impulsivity, making them particularly prone to taking overdoses or attempting suicide a lot sooner than people would expect.

Level 8: Because sevens are very expressive, you will begin to see them become more erratic and unstable. They won't be able to stop themselves from showing all their mood swings and impulses.

Level 7: They are working hard to control their mood swings, crushing anxieties, and lows, so they give themselves to all manner of things that can help in that regard. This makes them overindulge in alcohol, drugs, and other addictions that seem to have an effect on their mental state.

Average Levels

Level 6: They over-consume everything that they have become attached to. They may appear self-centered as they seem to put the things that give them the fix they need above everybody else. They are still unsatisfied, and this is the main source of their overindulgence.

Level 5: They have not yet figured out what the thing they need is, so they have a penchant to say yes to anything that can take their focus off their minds and transport them elsewhere. They can bury themselves in all sorts of activities that are absorbing. They become uninhibited and act in ways that are attention-seeking in a bid to keep themselves busy because they are desperate to escape their inner world.

Level 4: They still seem to be flooded with more choices than they can fathom. Their impulse to escape themselves makes them adventurous and experimentalist. They are on their way to becoming connoisseurs or refined consumers, so they keep themselves involved and informed of the latest trends in whatever sector stimulates their minds the most.

Healthy Levels

Level 3: Because they have such a diverse well of experiences, they can easily become successful in almost any field that they throw themselves into. They are notoriously flexible, and they work hard.

Level 2: They find themselves overjoyed by all things extroverted. They are happier, they are spontaneous, and they spread a lot of energy and enthusiasm wherever they find themselves.

Level 1: They are still very happy. Now they learn to find joy in the not so remarkable things in life. They are content, and they find pleasure in almost all experiences. They may be at their most thankful, having gone through so much and achieved such peace. That gratitude furthers their happiness and expands their appreciation of life in all its forms.

Type 8: The Challenger

Unhealthy Levels

Level 9: When faced with a difficult situation, they respond with force in a way that some might call barbaric, ruthless, or heartless. They teeter close to sociopathy and antisocial disorder. This is because their biggest fear is a loss of control, so they make threats in order to stay in command. They believe that responding with such force is the best way to do so.

Level 8: They believe themselves to be a lot more powerful than they generally are. They overestimate their influence. This is because they think when others cower around them that they have won, not realizing that they have only sown enemies.

Level 7: They refuse to be under the command, authority, or control of anyone even when that person rightfully expects it from them. They rebel and go anywhere where they can assert themselves. This is because they perceive any submission as a threat to their sense of self.

Average Levels

Level 6: They are combative in their relationships, whether it is work or personal relationships. They refuse to compromise in anything they do, perceiving doing so as a sign of surrender or weakness. They treat others badly as a way of asserting their power, finding that if they do so, others will easily fold when faced with them. Their reputation is of great importance to them. That is why they take every opportunity to inflate it. This is one way that their influence is propagated.

Level 5: They assert their dominance everywhere they go. But now they stop being intimidating. They resort to techniques that give them a better chance of winning the support of others. They have learned that being combative and intimidating are not sustainable ways of attaining control in the long run.

Level 4: They learn to become self-sufficient. They get serious about collecting as many resources in their lives that will afford them adequate control and power. Because the level of comfort they want is tied to being free, they may start their own business and work relentlessly at it even to the point of neglecting all their other needs.

Healthy Levels

Level 3: They are much more confident in their ways, and they have found their niche. Now they can be seen as being a natural leader having learned how to keep an advantageous balance between their more vicious side and their hard-working, more pragmatic side. They are always eager to take the position of power in any domain they find themselves in.

Level 2: They find in themselves a passion for many of the things they want, and they get them. They are less concerned about trying to control everything and being in power because they are confident that they have it. Wherever they find themselves, they will be fine. So they go into the work with a lot more confidence, grace, and gentleness.

Level 1: They are now masterful. They now have learned to tame themselves. They come across as merciful, courageous, and at the top of their game.

Type 9: The Peacemaker

Unhealthy Levels

Level 9: They have high levels of self-neglect. They are known for being disorientated and feel confused and bothered.

Level 8: Since they have so little peace inside of them, they try hard to protect the little peace they can muster. So they block out the troubles of the world around them and retreat inside. Because they shelter themselves, they cannot easily function within the word and the world can be overstimulating at times.

Level 7: They have a high sense of vulnerability; they feel like they cannot deal with any problems or conflicts that may arise. So they try their best to avoid conflict. They still find the world too rough for them.

Average Levels

Level 6: As a strategy to cope with feeling overloaded, they start to make things a lot less serious than they are - they minimize. They hope if they do so, they won't feel as threatened and that those around them will not respond in an unfavorable way to the situation. This method extends to people. They can become stubborn as well because they only know so many ways that work for them - they have too few coping mechanisms that others can understand.

Level 5: They begin to get involved, but they still appear to be removed, inattentive and withdrawn. They do this because they don't want to be affected when things turn sour; this aloofness and toe-in-the-water strategy serves that purpose. They refuse to be confrontational or deal with problems head-on, or even to bring up news that may be troubling; instead, they hide these issues as long as possible. They spend a lot of time thinking.

Level 4: They still fear getting into conflicts, so they become humble, reserved, and accommodating in their dealings with others. They are no longer aloof, but they refuse to assert their will, instead they go along with everybody else. At this point, everyone is happy to see them involved because that is much more comfortable to deal with. They conform easily, and when they find themselves in difficult situations, they deflect.

Healthy Levels

Level 3: They become more supportive of others, comfortable not to be in the limelight. They think a lot, so a very perceptive nine may offer great counsel to those in positions of power. They enjoy smoothing things over when people are in conflict, and they have exceptional negotiation skills, having learned to get what they want without being forceful.

Level 2: They are serene, and they are a well of harmony and peace.

Level 1: They find themselves satisfied and content; they look at the world with more awareness. They can form deep and strong relationships, and everywhere they go, they exude peace and stillness. They are connected to the present and others with great depth and intensity without losing sight of themselves.

Chapter 4: Self-Actualization

This chapter will explore what the different personality types have to do to get to self-actualization quickly.

Type 1: The Reformer

Ones need to realize that the world isn't entirely dependent on them for change to happen. They can rest and spend their energy elsewhere. It is okay to look after themselves first. The entire planet is the project of many; each one of us does something that counts in some big or small way. So play your part and don't overextend yourself.

You might feel that it is your place to tell others when they have done wrong or feel justified to show your anger and dissatisfaction. You need to learn that all of us have our shortcomings, and what you find easy and obvious may not come so easily to others, vice versa. So you need to practice a lot more patience with others. When you feel the need to be critical, think of something nice you can say about the person. Positive reinforcement is very encouraging, and it creates long-lasting relationships in the long run. That is what you need.

Let yourself be human; let yourself feel things and talk more openly about your emotions. This will foster deeper relationships with others in your life. It might be difficult to do so, but you have to realize that other people don't look at emotions or human nature in the same way you do. They aren't as quick to judge or find fault, so it is okay to confess and open up. It will make you a lot more just. If you find flaws in yourself, embrace them and do not be harsh on yourself, as this will allow you to better manage the issue.

Type 2: The Helper

You need to learn early that you should attend to your needs before you fulfill anyone else's. If you do this, you free yourself from feelings of resentment, anger, and entitlement. People who accept your help do so assuming that you are in an apt position to help; they are not privy to all of the sacrifices you make. So when you get angry with them for it, they see it as unfair to them because they wouldn't have asked you if they knew.

Whenever you get an urge to help someone, look at your motivations. If you expect something in return and it is appropriate to ask, make it clear. Otherwise, just help others because it is the right thing to do and it makes you happy. The sooner you learn that nobody owes you anything, the sooner you save yourself a lot of heartache, and you make yourself the source of all your happiness. Peoples are attracted to and love people who are happy with themselves.

Do not actively make others feel like they are in your debt, even if they are. Doing so only makes others around you feel bad, and they may withdraw from you.

Type 3: The Achiever

You work hard, and you might feel like this is the only thing that should matter, but it isn't. Allow yourself to take breaks and connect with the people in your life. It doesn't have to be something that takes up your entire day, a couple of texts or a phone call or sharing lunch with them will do. This will replenish your resources and allow you to grow into a more well-rounded individual who is successful on many fronts. It is no good to have things together in one area and not much in other areas in your life.

Don't try to impress others by being boastful and showy, this only drives other people away from you or ruins the substance of your relationship with them. The fruits of your labor will speak for themselves. Try to be authentic and down to earth, and don't hide behind grand ideas about who you are and what you have achieved. Learn to cooperate with others and to be involved in a social project. This will help you find yourself.

Type 4: The Individualist

Don't let yourself be purely driven by your feelings. You should do things even when you are not in the mood to do them because doing this will help reveal your nature to yourself, as you will be outside the confines of your emotions. I say this because fours often confuse how they feel with who they are, but feelings aren't your identity, they are events that happen to you. To grow, you need to find out who you are outside their bonds.

Learn to take on new challenges even if you feel that you are not ready or you are ill-prepared. It is the only way you will develop full confidence in yourself and grow. You should think about cutting down on how much you drink or self-indulge as these things negatively affect you. Sometimes you are not doing well because you are incapable, and it is unhealthy habits that are holding you back.

Type 5: The Investigator

You can be indecisive since you can see many ways a situation could devolve. It can be helpful to accelerate your decision-making process. Find someone whose judgment you trust and ask them to give you advice. In the end, you must be comfortable with the fact that there aren't any perfect decisions. The best you can do is make decisions with fewer disadvantages. Find confidence in the fact that you can't make too many bad decisions in a row, so if you find that you have made one you can get out of it - it is not the end of the world.

You should allow yourself to calm down and quiet your mind. So finding activities that help you do this is important. It can be easy to resort to drugs and alcohol to achieve this, but these substances are not good for your self-esteem or sense of well-being. They bypass your thorough decision-making process, so you find yourself having made decisions you would not normally make, and this can hurt you. Use substances in careful moderation or not at all. Meditation could prove very beneficial for you. Learn to rein yourself in and not let yourself be sucked in by where your curiosity takes you.

Type 6: The Loyalist

Anxiety is a huge problem for you. You always feel like something can go wrong even when things look to be right. This feeling of unrest is something that you need to learn not to run away from. You need to realize that most of the things you worry about do not happen at all. For instance, you can just jot down the things that you worry about in a journal. Then go back to look at which of the things that have worried you have come true, and you will see very few have. You might say, "Not yet." But this misses the point; when you are anxious, you are anxious that the thing will happen at any moment. You should ask yourself, if it hasn't happened since then, what is the use of living like it just might?

You should learn to calm yourself in a healthy way; drugs and alcohol will only worsen your situation as they can destabilize your mind. You should learn to trust others; if you find it hard, it might be that the people around you don't inspire trust, so find someone who does. While not everyone inspires much trust, most people deserve at least some, so learn to delegate and trust others. This will make you feel a lot lighter.

Type 7: The Enthusiast

Your biggest issue is your impulsiveness. You should try to observe your impulses, experience them as they are, and let them pass. The aim of this is for you to realize you do not have to act on every one. Learn to do things in moderation. Try practicing more delayed gratification; you do not always have to have what you want when you want it. These small habits will help you discover yourself because you won't be too busy immersing yourself in whatever catches your eye.

Type 8: The Challenger

You do not always have to be in control of situations. Learn to give others space and a chance to control things, and give them the autonomy they deserve. You won't be suited to take the lead in every situation. Not everyone who seems to get in your way is against you. In general, people have good intentions, so try to find the good reasons why people in your life do what they do. You should resist the urge to be threatening and confrontational, above all, it will not get you what you want. This strategy is not useful in the long run; life is a marathon, not a sprint.

Type 9: The Peacemaker

It won't hurt to be honest about your feelings and tell people what you want even if it may upset things. Not all conflict is bad, and not all of it will lead to disaster – some of it is an opportunity for growth. Only when you open yourself up to that idea will you start having nourishing relationships in your life. You should be confident that if a conflict arises, your peaceful nature is competent enough to deal with it. You have to become more open, and you will see that the world is a lot kinder and more welcoming to your nature than you think.

Conclusion

As I have promised, our journey was short but not without useful information. I hope that the guidance I have provided you will prove useful as you journey through life and self-discovery.

If You Enjoyed This Book In Anyway, An Honest Review Is Always Appreciated!

www.ingramcontent.com/pod-product-compliance
Lightning Source LLC
Chambersburg PA
CBHW030347050426
42336CB00048B/510